The Manger Where Jesus Lay

"This will be
a sign to you:
You will find
a baby
wrapped in cloths
and lying in a manger."

Luke 2:12

The Standard Publishing Company, Cincinnati, Ohio
A division of Standex International Corporation
© 1996 by The Standard Publishing Company
8121 Hamilton Avenue, Cincinnati, Ohio 45231
All rights reserved. Printed in U.S.A.
03 02 01 00 99 98 97 96   5 4 3 2 1

STANDARD
PUBLISHING
Cincinnati, Ohio

MARTHA LARCHAR

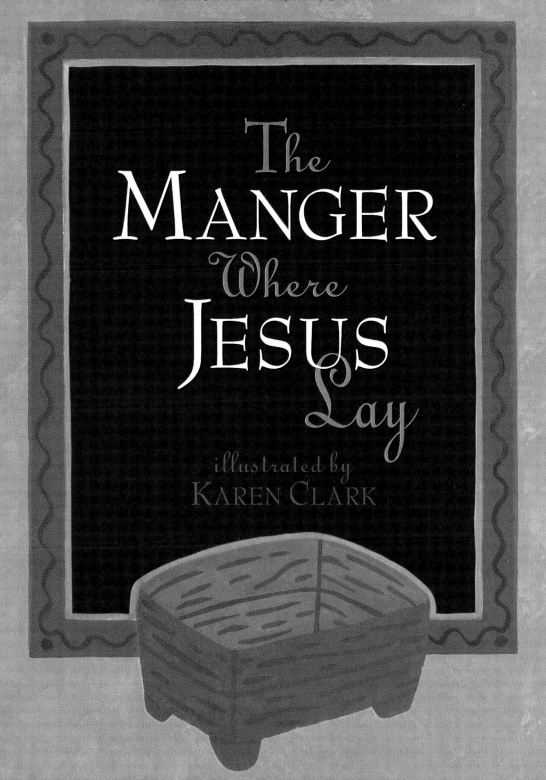

The
MANGER
Where
JESUS
Lay

illustrated by
KAREN CLARK

Manger

This is the  where Jesus lay.

Hay

These are the bundles of sweet-smelling

that filled the  where Jesus lay.

Cows

These are the 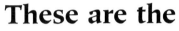 all gathered 'round,

who ate the bundles of sweet-smelling

that filled the  where Jesus lay.

Stable

This is the  safe and sound,

home for the  all gathered 'round,

who ate the bundles of sweet-smelling

that filled the  where Jesus lay.

Night

This is the  so dark and cold,

outside the 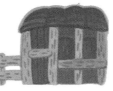 safe and sound,

home for the  all gathered 'round,

who ate the bundles of sweet-smelling

that filled the  where Jesus lay.

Star

This is the so bright and bold,

that shone in the  so dark and cold,

outside the 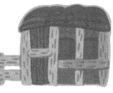 safe and sound,

home for the  all gathered 'round,

who ate the bundles of sweet-smelling

that filled the  where Jesus lay.

Angels

These are the  from heaven above,

up with the so bright and bold,

that shone in the  so dark and cold,

outside the  safe and sound,

home for the  all gathered 'round,

who ate the bundles of sweet-smelling

that filled the  where Jesus lay.

Shepherds

These are the who heard of God's love,

sung by the  from heaven above,

up with the so bright and bold,

that shone in the so dark and cold,

around the  safe and sound,

home for the  all gathered 'round,

who ate the bundles of sweet-smelling

that filled the where Jesus lay.

Then Mary and Joseph, rejoicing and glad,

greeted the Shepherds who heard of God's love,

sung by the Angels from heaven above,

up with the Star so bright and bold,

that shone in the Night so dark and cold,

outside the Stable safe and sound,

home for the Cows all gathered 'round,

who ate the bundles of sweet-smelling Hay . . .

and knelt by the Manger where Jesus lay.

Match these words with the pictures.

baby Jesus

hay

angels

night

shepherds

cows

stable

manger

star

Mary and Joseph

Now find the pictures wherever they appear in the rest of the book.